COLOURS, SHAPES AND SIZES

© 1987 GRANDREAMS LIMITED

First published 1987. This edition published 1990.

Written and illustrated by Anne & Ken McKie.

Published by
GRANDREAMS LIMITED,
Jadwin House, 205/211 Kentish Town Road, London NW5 2JU.

Printed in Belgium   RB3-4

Learn about
COLOURS

This bear is yellow.

This bear is red.

This bear is blue.

Colours can be mixed together to make other colours.

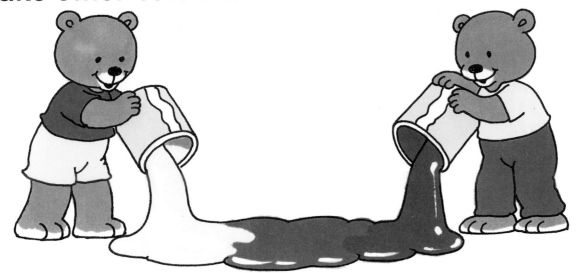

Yellow and red make orange.

Yellow and blue make green.

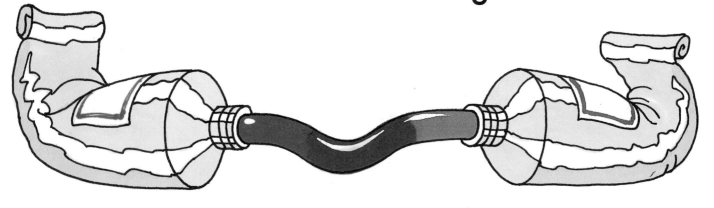

Red and blue make purple.

You can paint a picture in just
black and white.

Or in lots of lovely colours.

Here are some things that are yellow.

Here are some things that are red.

Here are some things that are blue.

Here are some things that are green.

Here are some things that are different colours.

How many different colours can you count on this page?

Colour in stripes and spots.

Here is a picture for you to colour.

Learn about
SHAPES

This is a circle.

This is a triangle.

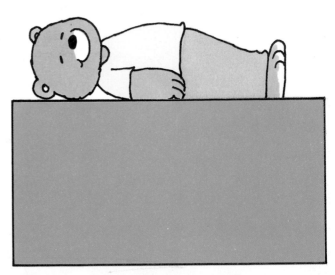

This is a square.

This is a rectangle.

Look for the circles in this picture.

There are lots of triangles in this picture.

This picture has lots of squares.

Can you find all the rectangles?

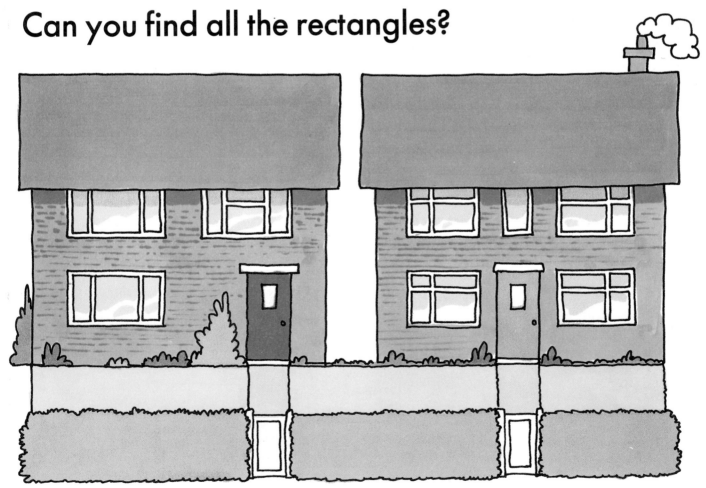

Can you name the shapes on the bed covers?

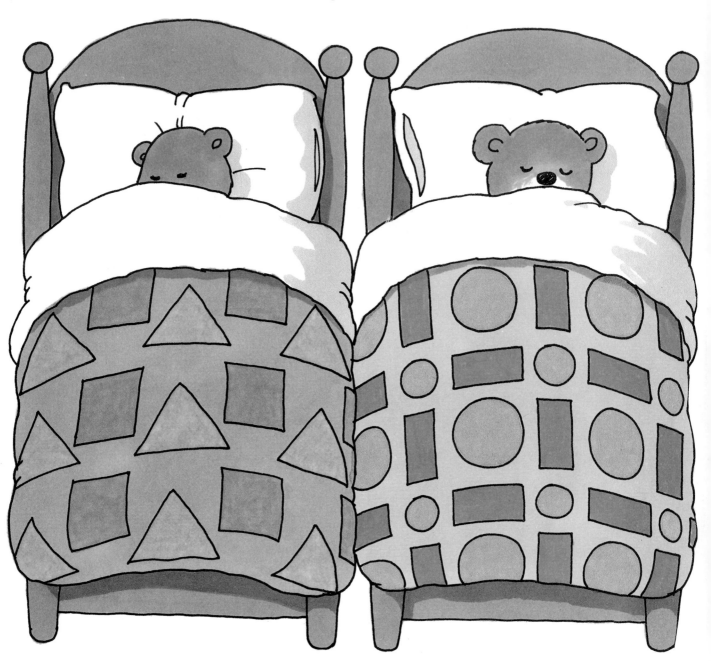

The bears are wearing the shapes.

Can you see which shapes would fit the holes in the boxes?

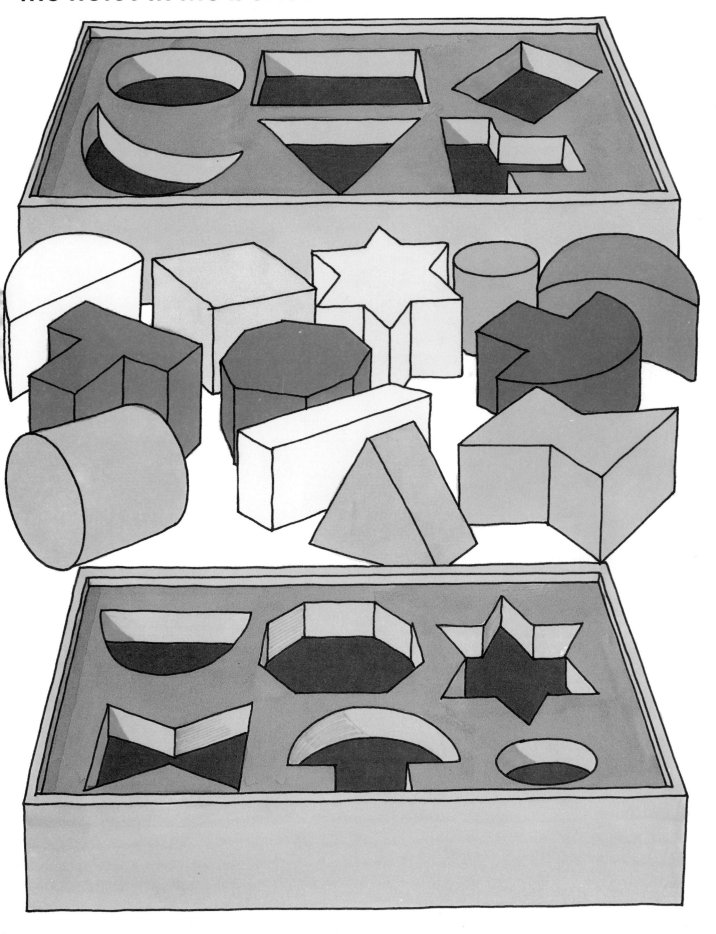

Here are small shapes that have been built to make one big shape.

Can you guess what these shapes are?
You can see what they are on the next page.

Now you can see what was on the last page. Did you guess right?

Making shapes with plasticine.

Drawing around shapes.

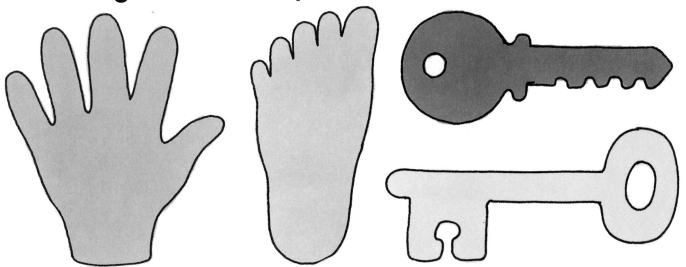

Making pictures with paper shapes.

Learn about SIZES

I am big.
He is bigger.

I am small.

She is smaller.

Do you know how big you are?

From big to little.

Big things.

Small things.

Which ball is the biggest?

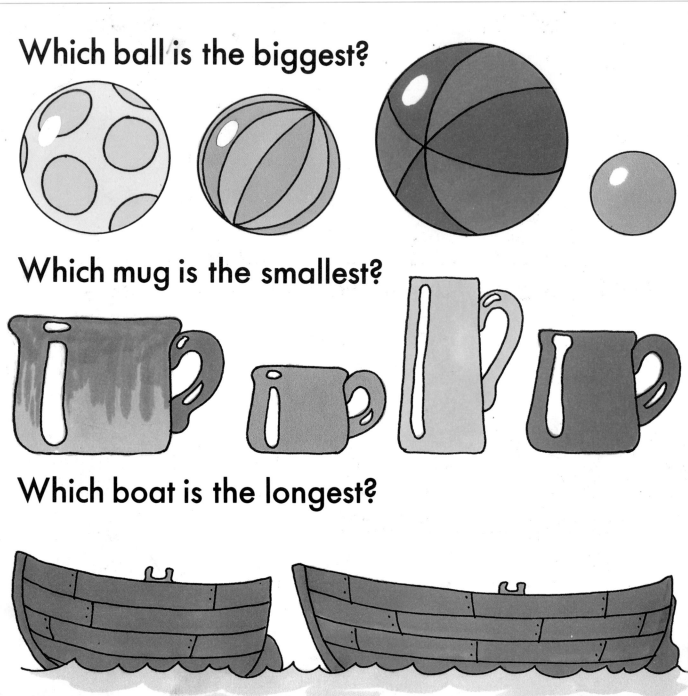

Which mug is the smallest?

Which boat is the longest?

Which pencil is the thinnest?